Benjamin Apthorp Gould

Eulogy on Joseph S. Hubbard

Benjamin Apthorp Gould

Eulogy on Joseph S. Hubbard

ISBN/EAN: 9783337329778

Printed in Europe, USA, Canada, Australia, Japan

Cover: Foto ©Thomas Meinert / pixelio.de

More available books at **www.hansebooks.com**

EULOGY ON JOSEPH S. HUBBARD.

By B. A. GOULD.

EULOGY

JOSEPH S. HUBBARD.

By B. A. GOULD.

[Read before the National Academy at New Haven, 1864, Aug. 5.]

MR. PRESIDENT AND GENTLEMEN : —

The Constitution of our Academy, like the organic law of most Academies of Science beyond the seas, provides for the tribute of a formal Biographical Notice, pronounced in open session, in commemoration of each of our number who may be removed by death. For it is no unreasonable assumption that public benefit and individual incentives may be derived from the history of any man whose scientific services have rendered him worthy of admittance to your number.

It has been the will of God that the first place in our ranks made vacant by death should be that of JOSEPH STILLMAN HUBBARD, and in obedience to your instructions I am here to tell the simple story of his life ; — not without a doubt of my own ability for the task, yet glad that the lot has fallen to my share, for none outside the narrow limits of his kindred could have held him dearer.

Upon our roll, Gentlemen of the Academy, are the names of venerable men, whose usefulness has extended through a period surpassing the total duration of most human lives, and side by side with these are the names of others, who were not yet cradled when the former were full of honors, and crowned with gray hairs. The years of our eldest and youngest member differ by more than half a century. Yet the first summons came, not to any of the great masters in science who give its lustre to the new gem with which an afflicted but regenerate land would fain crown her aching brows; not to those who might well claim to have finished the work on earth, which their talents and opportunities seemed to mark out for them; — it came to one of the youngest in our ranks, — the forty-sixth of the original fifty in order of age, — to one whose work seemed chiefly in the future, and from whom we expected bright laurels for the Academy and for America.

When in April, 1863, we assembled for the great work of founding a National Academy, none was more hopeful, none more buoyant, none more impressed with the magnitude and import of our new duties, than he. It was the realization of the dream of his maturer years, the new Atlantis of his scientific aspiration, and his heart was full of bright anticipations, tinged with all the hues which a noble enthusiasm could bestow.

"A better Three Days for science were never spent," he wrote to his brother; and to his pastor in Washington, "The inauguration of this Academy marks the most important epoch ever witnessed by Science in America; — *we* say in the world."

In less than four months after that meeting in New York, his generous, fervid heart had ceased to beat. He died 1863, August 16, twenty-one days before the completion of his fortieth year.

The custom has always seemed to me an eminently proper one, which prefaces the history of a life by some mention and notice of ancestry. For, — whether we adopt the European notion that the ancestor ennobles his descendant by

good deeds, or the perhaps more equitable Asiatic idea that
honor flows in an ascending course, ennobling those whose
nurturing care has thus borne fruit, — the bond of lineage
may not lightly be disregarded ; and each day's experience
teaches us anew, that " men do not gather grapes of thorns
nor figs of thistles."

I may therefore say that our departed colleague drew his
origin from the early founders of our race, from that sturdy
stock which gave character to the Colony of Massachusetts
Bay, and shaped the civilization of New England.

His first American ancestor, Mr. WILLIAM HUBBARD,
came out at the age of forty in the " Defence " from London, in the year 1635, and soon established himself in Ipswich, Essex County, Massachusetts ; which town he represented for eight successive years, from 1638 to 1646, in the
Legislature of the Colony. In 1662, he removed to Boston,
where he died in the year 1670, aged seventy-five years,
leaving three sons, all born in England.

The eldest of these sons and second in the line of descent
was the Rev. WILLIAM HUBBARD, a man of much note in
his day. Born in 1622, he was but thirteen years old when
his father brought him to the new world. He graduated at
Harvard College in 1642, and was in 1658 ordained colleague of Rev. THOMAS COBBETT in Ipswich, where he remained as pastor until his death in 1704; his kinsman, Rev.
JOHN ROGERS, son of the President of Harvard College,
acting as his colleague during the later years of his life.

This learned and good man was one of the first historians
of the early troubles with the Indians. Two works on this
subject were published by him in 1677, and subsequently
republished in London in one volume under the title, " The
Present State of New England." His " History of New
England," left by him in manuscript, is preserved in the ar-

2

chives of the Massachusetts Historical Society, and forms volumes V. and VI. of their printed " Collections." In 1688, after the departure of President INCREASE MATHER for England, he was commissioned by Governor ANDROS to officiate as President or Rector at the Harvard Commencement, being the oldest clerical Alumnus in New England ; and as there were no graduates in that year, it is recorded in Sewall's Diary that he delivered an oration on the occasion, although this has not been transmitted to us.* His first wife, and the mother of his children, was Margaret, daughter of Rev. NATHANIEL ROGERS, and said to have been the great-granddaughter of that JOHN ROGERS who was burnt at the stake in Smithfield, 1555, — although, according to that accurate investigator, Mr. SAVAGE, this claim is not well substantiated.

---

* That Rev. WILLIAM HUBBARD was a man of no small independence and decision of character, may easily be inferred from his works ; but other indications of his mental and moral force are not wanting. In the ecclesiastical troubles of 1667, connected with the establishment of the " Old South Church " in Boston, he took strong ground and bore an active part ; and on the passage of a vote of censure upon himself and his colleagues in 1670, by a committee of the Legislature, he was one of the number who answered with a protest of such ability and convincing force, that the Legislature replied by an ample apology.

John Dunton, who visited him in 1686, gives [Felt, Hist. Ipswich, p. 230] the following description of Mr. Hubbard : " The benefit of nature and the fatigue of study have equally contributed to his eminence. Neither are we less obliged to both than himself ; he freely communicates of his learning to all who have the happiness to share in his converse. In a word, he is learned without ostentation and vanity, and gives all his productions such a delicate turn and grace, ... that the features and lineaments of the child make a clear discovery and distinction of the father ; yet he is a man of singular modesty, of strict morals, and has done as much for the conversion of the Indians as most men in New England."

The several successive generations of our colleague's ancestors seem to have been, without exception, men of moral worth, and of influence in the community.

Rev. JOHN HUBBARD, in the fourth generation, was settled in 1698 at Jamaica, Long Island, where he was distinguished by a Christian charity and tolerance remarkable for those days. His son JOHN settled in New Haven, where he served the community in the various capacities of physician, Colonel, Representative, Judge of Probate, and Judge of Common Pleas ; and his descendants have continued to reside in the vicinity of this beautiful and classic city.*

Here our colleague was born, 1823, Sept. 7 (in the ninth generation from the American founder of his family), being

* The line of descent is as follows : —
I. WILLIAM, b. in England, 1595 ; d. Ipswich, Mass., 1670.
II. Rev. WILLIAM, b. England, 1622 (H. C. 1642); d. Ipswich, 1794, Sept. 14 ; married Margaret, daughter of Rev. Nathaniel Rogers.
III. JOHN, a merchant of Boston, b. Ipswich, 1648; d. 1710, Jan. 8 ; married Ann, daughter of Gov. John Leverett.
IV. Rev. JOHN, of Jamaica, N. Y., b. Boston, 1677, Jan. 9 (H. C. 1695); d. 1705, Oct. 5. [See Thompson, Hist. of Long Island, 1st ed., p. 388; also Boston News Letter, No. 79, 1705, Oct. 22.]
V. Dr. JOHN, of New Haven, b. Jamaica, 1703, Nov. 30 (A. M. Yale, 1730) ; d. 1773, Oct. 30 ; married 1724, Elizabeth Stevens.
VI. Rev. JOHN, of Meriden, Conn., b. New Haven, 1727, Jan. 24 (Y. C. 1744); d. 1786, Nov. 18 ; married 1750, Jan. 25, Rebecca Dickerman. [See Meriden Historical Collections.]
VII. ISAAC, of Meriden, b. Meriden, 1752, Nov. 22 ; married 1782, Dec. 5, Jane, daughter of Thomas Berry.
VIII. EZRA STILES, of New Haven, b. Meriden, 1794, May 13 ; d. 1861, Aug. 20 ; married 1820, Dec. 13, Eliza, daughter of Josiah Church.
IX. JOSEPH STILLMAN, of Washington, D.C., b. New Haven, 1823, Sept. 7 (Y. C. 1843).

the second son of EZRA STILES HUBBARD, and ELIZA
CHURCH of New Haven, — parents to whom he was more
than tenderly attached, and whose declining years were
blessed by his thoughtful devotion. Of his father, I may
quote his own words written three years ago : " My father
has done his life's work well. Unable from feeble health to
live the scholar's life to which he had been destined by his
uncle, President STILES, and honoring learning next to god-
liness, he endeavored to give his children every advantage
attainable for scholarship, devoting his life, labors, and scanty
means to this one object. Precious is his memory."

From a most interesting and touching sketch of his early
life, prepared by his admirable mother, I may be permitted
to gather some of the incidents of his boyhood illustrative of
the peculiar traits of his character, — earnestness, enthusiasm, and self-forgetfulness, modified by a wholesome love of
fun and frolic, a tender susceptibility, and an affectionate
nature. From the whole account it is manifest that in .
childhood as in maturer life he made for himself a place
in the hearts of all with whom he came in contact ; and I
think it may be said of him with literal truth, what is so
rarely true even of good men endowed with far less force of
character, that he had not an enemy in the world.

With him, too, the old and ever new experience came to
his parents, of the early yearning of an intellectual child
for books and knowledge, and they afterwards lamented
that this dangerous tendency was not more carefully held in
check. But although the danger of over-stimulating a recep-
tive brain can hardly be exaggerated, and though the pre-
cautions of physical education were at that time comparatively disregarded among us, — I see no reason for suspicion
of any morbid precocity. I venture to make the following
extracts from the interesting accounts kindly furnished me
by his mother : —

" In his eighth year he suffered a severe course of lung fever, and for several weeks after the crisis was past seemed vacillating between life and death. After he began to convalesce, it was almost impossible to keep his active mind quiet enough to suffer the weakened frame to recover its tone. Pictures, books, toys, everything we could devise, were put into requisition to amuse him. His father saw one day in a store a curious piece of mechanism, a puzzle which he knew would delight the child, — but it was an expensive article, and he hesitated if he ought to purchase it. But a second thought of the tired, weary boy decided the question. When he put it into Joseph's hand, as he sat bolstered up in bed, the child's eyes fairly flashed with delight. Seeing him so much amused at studying its intricacies, I left him, ... and returning after a while found him utterly exhausted. He had taken the toy to pieces to ascertain its construction, and in trying to put it together again, had so used the little strength he had gained as to leave us for many days to fear a fatal result. That was ever one of his peculiarities, — not to rest till he understood the how and why of everything he saw, or at least had learned all that could be learned about it. . . . . It was about his ninth year that he began especially to develop his peculiar taste for mathematical studies and mechanics. Though he loved play dearly, and enjoyed it with zest for a little while, he had far rather spend his hours out of school in trying experiments, endeavoring to make machines, &c. . . . One of his great efforts was to make a clock. He had been attracted by seeing his father wind up the time-piece, and had begged to examine it. A day or two after I found him in his room, surrounded by a quaint collection of bits of board, pasteboard, wire, lead, &c. To the question, ' What is the tinker about now?' he replied: 'Mother, I'm going to make a

2 *

clock.' I told him we must ask his father for some tools, and perhaps he would succeed; and he did succeed, — constructing a clock in all its parts, with face, hands, &c., and which went for a time, being duly mounted on the kitchen shelf, and for making which his only tools were a pair of scissors and a jackknife.

"After that, his father procured him a small chest of tools, and from that day he had full employment for every leisure hour. The attic was appropriated for his wood-work, and the back piazza for his crucibles, castings, &c. Most of his leisure time before entering college was devoted to making a telescope, which proved to be quite a good instrument, and which he sold to a gentleman from Catskill, soon after he entered college. He made also a camera-obscura, which afforded a fund of amusement to himself and his playmates, and a press for binding books. As long as his father lived he used the blank books with which the boy supplied him at this time.

"When fitting for college, while visiting some mechanic's shop, in pursuit of material or instruction, he came in contact with EBENEZER MASON, who was then one of Yale's enthusiastic astronomers, and at once there sprung up between the young man and the boy a kindly sympathy. MASON introduced the lad to his own chosen associates in study, invited him to their rooms for work, experiments, &c.; and from that day his scientific life began in earnest. Nothing could make him so happy as permission to spend the evening he could spare from daily lessons with MASON and HAMILTON SMITH; and, when in college, to be invited to watch shooting-stars or take observations with Mr. HERRICK, was the greatest boon the world could afford him. His standing in college was above mediocrity, but not what he could easily have made it. His mind was so entirely filled with his own loved department of study, that he did not value college honors enough to give the needful attention to other branches.

"In his sixteenth year Joseph determined to take a pedestrian excursion. He set out to visit an uncle residing twenty or thirty miles north of us, and his father furnished him with all he thought needful for so short a trip. He had always kept us informed of his movements when away; and when six days had passed, and we received no intelligence from him, we began to be seriously uneasy. At length a letter came, mailed in Charlestown, Mass. He had heard MASON and SMITH talk about a mechanic in Ware, who had given them much information about casting mirrors for telescopes, and had long wished to see the man for himself. So, after tarrying one night at his uncle's, he had wended his way up to Ware, and having learned all he could from the man he sought, had proceeded on foot to Charlestown, a distance of 175 miles, in order to visit Bunker Hill."

In 1843, he graduated at Yale College. For a few months he remained at home pursuing his favorite studies, mathematics and astronomy; and in the following winter he taught for a while in a classical school. Early in 1844, he went to Philadelphia, as an assistant of WALKER, who was then beginning his astronomical labors, and whose attention had been attracted by the bright promise of the earnest and gifted youth. Here the contagious zeal of WALKER added fuel to the flame. Removed for the first time from the restraining influence of home, on which he had learned unconsciously to depend, he forgot all prudent care for himself. He observed with WALKER at the High-School Observatory all night, and computed all the day, — and I need not add that his health soon gave way. From that time he was subject to a nervous excitability before unknown to him, and to an irregular action of the heart, from which he suffered much, and which finally exhausted his strength and energies, — depriving him of that vigor of constitution with which he was originally endowed, and which might have arrested the progress of his last disease.

In the autumn of 1844, Lieut. (now Major General) FRÉMONT offered Mr. HUBBARD a position in Washington as computer of the observations for latitude and longitude made on his expeditions across the Rocky Mountains, and on the Pacific coast. These completed, and the interest of Prof. BACHE, Capt. FRÉMONT, and Col. BENTON being enlisted in his behalf by his successful and meritorious labors in Philadelphia and Washington, they obtained a promise from Mr. BANCROFT, then Secretary of the Navy, that his appointment should immediately be made out for a vacancy in the corps of Professors of Mathematics in the Navy. He was commissioned 1845, May 7, and immediately assigned to duty at the Washington Observatory, of which he continued an officer during the remainder of his life. He was elected a member of the National Institute of Washington, 1845, January 14; of the Connecticut Academy of Arts and Sciences, 1849, October 24; of the American Academy of Arts and Sciences in Boston, 1850, August 15; and of the American Philosophical Society of Philadelphia, 1852, May 7.

It would be needless, gentlemen of the Academy, did taste not forbid, for me to describe to you at any length, the embarrassments of astronomers, stationed at the Washington Observatory, while under the charge of the late Superintendent. Few of you, if any, can have failed to appreciate the painful conflict between self-respect and official proprieties, — between the emotions of the scientist, jealous of his country's reputation, and of the subordinate, whose duty in an establishment under military organization demanded tacit submission and apparent acquiescence, under a mortifying or atrocious policy. The sensitive nature of WALKER found it impossible to endure the trial; but his pupil, HUBBARD, struggled more successfully.

Would that I might with propriety express my keen sense of the deep debt of gratitude due from American science to those able and disinterested men, some of them, happily, still of our number, who bore the mortifications of their position without flinching, that they might save the national scientific institution, which it was partially within their power to protect, from becoming a source of national disgrace. They toiled earnestly and judiciously for the sake of their hope that some small portion of their labor might bear fruit, though that fruit should not be plucked by them. They struggled against obstacles which would have deterred most men, in order that the noble instruments might render some service to science, or at least fail to be made implements of national disgrace. How well they succeeded, their record bears witness; and it will bear eternal testimony to their honor, when in its own good time history shall break the seals which the present day has necessarily affixed.

A single anecdote from many which might be told, illustrative of the state of things, may perhaps be pardonable now, although it would never have been publicly mentioned by our departed colleague, nor with his permission.

Professor HUBBARD was one morning summoned to the presence of the Superintendent, who handed him a letter just received from Germany, and desired its translation. It contained the announcement of the discovery of a new comet, together with observations of its position on two successive days, — an interval of eighteen or twenty days having of course elapsed since that time.

"I wish an Ephemeris of this comet," said he, "to be prepared without delay, for publication in the newspaper to-morrow morning." HUBBARD respectfully suggested that three observations were requisite for computing the elements, and that even should the comet be found early in the evening, the intervals between the three dates would not be well adapted for the purpose. "Confound the elements, Mr. HUBBARD!" said the Lieutenant, using some rather strong expletives; "I want none of your Elements, I only want an Ephemeris, and I wish you would compute it at once."

What the astronomer did under the embarrassing circumstances, I do not exactly know ; but I suspect that the Ephemeris, which went to the *National Intelligencer*, was computed by methods neither of OLBERS nor of BESSEL!

The first published observations of HUBBARD, so far as I am aware, were those by which, on the 4th of February, 1847, he confirmed the prediction of WALKER as to the identity of *Neptune* with one of the stars observed by LALANDE, 1795, May 10. This important discovery was made almost simultaneously by PETERSEN in Altona, and by WALKER and HUBBARD in Washington, and was of the highest importance for the accurate determination of the planet's orbit. By the employment of this ancient observation, and of the perturbations computed by PEIRCE, WALKER was enabled to deduce the orbit of *Neptune* with a precision which leaves even now very little to be desired, and which surpasses that attained by any other computer to this present day.

At the Naval Observatory HUBBARD was at once placed at the Transit-Instrument, with which he observed for four months ; and was transferred to the Meridian Circle in September. Nearly nine hundred transit-observations by him may be found in the volume of Washington Observations for

1845 ; and examination has shown them to possess decided value, in spite of the very unfavorable circumstances under which they were made. During the remainder of the year he was occupied with the adjustments, and in determining the Instrumental errors, of the Meridian Circle. The thorough description of this instrument and discussion of its corrections, in the volume for 1846, is from his pen ; as also is the description of the Prime-Vertical Transit. Nearly one thousand observations with the Meridian Circle in 1846, as well as the discussion already cited, give token of his activity ; but the equal labor of endeavoring to train and instruct many others, — who were assigned to duty at the several astronomical instruments by the naval routine, although not inclined to astronomical pursuits, and indeed often affected with distaste for them, — does not appear. Nor is any mention made of the careful and laborious organization and inception of a system of zone-observations, admirably devised and arranged by one of our present colleagues in connection with Professor HUBBARD, although no public acknowledgement of their services in this respect was ever made, nor indeed claimed, by either of them. According to the plan of these zone-observations (Washington Observations, 1845, App., p. 32), the micrometers of the Mural Circle, Transit-Instrument, and Meridian Circle were provided with additional declination-threads; additional transit-threads were inserted in the field of the Mural Circle, and the micrometer of the Transit-Instrument was rotated $90°$; thus rendering it available for the measure of differences of declination. The several zones were made to overlap by $10'$ in declination, and the instruments were to be employed simultaneously upon nearly the same declination, so that a portion of the stars observed by the Mural and Transit should be identical. Thus the Transit-Instrument would give standard observations of right-ascensions for an adequate number of stars in each zone swept by the Mural Circle ; while this latter would in its turn give accurate declinations for a sufficient number of stars to determine the zones observed with the Transit. The Meridian Circle, meanwhile, was to go over the same ground independently, and thus all discordances which might arise from inevitable errors of observation would be satisfactorily disposed of.

These zone-observations were begun early in 1846, and continued till 1850, and even later ; and a large amount of material was thus collected. The zones observed during 1846 with the Meridian Circle were reduced and published (under the superintendence of Mr. FERGUSON of the Washington Observatory) in 1860 ; a portion of the Mural zones for 1846 had been reduced under the superintendence of Professor COFFIN before he left the Observatory, and a considerable amount of labor had been given by HUBBARD to the reduction of the Transit-zones for the same year. With these exceptions, nothing had been done toward the reduction, on the accession of the present Superintendent in 1861 ; although in the mean time a similar investigation had been planned by Professor ARGELANDER, completely executed by him over all the practicable region south of Bessel's limit, and with a single instrument, and the results published in 1852, under the title of " Southern Zones."

But although the great labor bestowed by COFFIN and HUBBARD on the arrangement and execution of this grand scheme proved in a great degree futile, — by reason of the neglect of the observations after they were made, by the loss of some of them, and by the reckless manner in which a large proportion of the work was done, — the value of the plan and ingenuity of the arrangement remain the same. Had the valuable and delicate instruments, and the execution of the work, remained in charge of astronomers, — rather than of gentlemen, who, however gallant and accomplished in their proper calling as lieutenants and midshipmen, could not reasonably be expected to do the work of astronomers without the requisite training, and frequently much to their distaste, — had the large sums·annually voted by Congress for the support of the Observatory been in part devoted to the reduction of these observations, and to the detection of the errors lurking in the observing books, — they would have conferred high honor upon American science, and indeed formed by far the noblest achievement of practical astronomy in America. As it is, it has been found necessary to reject all the zone-observations made since 1849 ; the remainder consist of a curious combination of observations of the most delicate character and conscientious accuracy, with others which are literally beyond criticism ; and the disregard of the original plan, and total lack of system in carrying on the work with the different instruments, has in great measure defeated the scheme, which prescribed that the same region should be swept by the Transit and the Mural. Thus the zones, when reduced, do not form a complete catalogue for the region over which they extend. Moreover, it has been found necessary to determine the zero-points, both for right-ascension and for declination, of a large proportion of the zones by observations of stars made during the last two years, at an expenditure of labor quite comparable with that of the original observations of the zones, and yet exposed to all the deleterious influences which may be exerted by the unknown proper motion of the comparison-stars during an interval of from fifteen to eighteen years. The reduction of these zones has been essentially completed, so that their publication may be looked for at no distant day ; and of this work a portion of the original excellent organization,

3

a considerable part of the earlier zones observed with the Meridian Circle, and two thirds of all the good work done with that instrument, is due to HUBBARD.

Still, in my desire to do full honor to the generous and gifted man whose loss we mourn, I may not do injustice to the living; and at the hazard of incurring the disapproval of a colleague, happily spared to us, I must add, that for an amount of intellectual labor bestowed upon this work, greater even than HUBBARD's, and for the exquisite elegance with which the observations with the Mural Circle were elaborated and made to give character and finish to the whole work, we are indebted to Professor COFFIN, whose transfer from the Observatory to the Naval Academy was productive of more advantage to the latter institution than to the one from which, unfortunately for its welfare, he was taken away in 1853. Still his influence and example were not lost, and to Professor YARNALL we owe an ample series of admirable observations with the Mural Circle, which, in connection with those of Mr. FERGUSON at the Equatorial, saved the honor of a national institution, at the time when HUBBARD was precluded by his health from observing, and after the departure of COFFIN; and have furnished valuable observations in an unbroken line from this well-equipped establishment down to the time of its resuscitation under the original founder, Capt. GILLISS.

The most valuable of HUBBARD's observations were unquestionably those with the Prime-Vertical Transit Instrument. This is essentially the counterpart of the one originally designed by STRUVE, and which has rendered such service at Pulkowa. It was thoroughly studied and mastered by HUBBARD soon after his appointment at the Observatory, and the scientific portions of the descriptions of the instrument were from the first chiefly from his pen.

It was not, however, till the beginning of 1848, a year and
a half after observations with the Prime-Vertical Instrument
had been commenced, that he was officially assigned to its
charge. The attainment of some definite result concerning
the long mooted annual parallax of *a Lyræ*, which passes
within 15' of the zenith of Washington, was an especially
cherished problem. For many years he labored towards
its solution, in spite of serious and most vexatious obstacles.
But the maxima and minima of the annual parallax occur
at seasons very unfavorable to observations in the climate
and atmosphere of Washington ; and it was chiefly due to
this fact, that some result was not long since attained. At
the regeneration of the Observatory in 1861, he was again
full of hopefulness and confidence of an early solution of
this favorite problem, as well as sundry others. " Your
rejoicing," he wrote, " cannot exceed mine ; for it is a con-
stant gratification to see order quenching chaos, energy
overriding the old slowness, and above all our own science
raising her triumphant head, and banishing the old humbug." Even at that period of his domestic bereavement
and loneliness, it needed only the unwonted consciousness
that Astronomy might be protected at the only national
Observatory in the land, to reanimate his spirits, and give
him a new stimulus to exertion. The Prime-Vertical Instrument, like the others, was soon put into complete order,
and the traces of early misuse thoroughly removed ; and in
March, 1862, he began a new series of observations of
a Lyræ. During the period of this series HUBBARD completed an exhaustive discussion of the influence of irregu-
larity of pivots upon the level-reading at different altitudes ;
— a determination of the effect and amount of flexure by
comparisons of the error of collimation deduced from re-
versing the telescope on a star with that resulting from

reversals on the image of the threads reflected from mercury in the nadir. He had re-determined the value of the level divisions, had removed some serious discordances arising from a faulty construction of the level, and had completed tables for the more convenient reduction of the observations.

This series of observations he intended to continue for several years, but an overruling Providence willed otherwise. His last observation was on the 8th of July, 1863, not sixteen months after the first. Happily he was favored with an able and skilful collaborator in Professor WILLIAM HARKNESS, and found a worthy successor. The series is continued by Professor NEWCOMB, than whom none is more competent to carry out the plans of his lamented associate, with all the success that scientific ability or earnest devotion can insure.

Professor NEWCOMB has investigated the probable error of HUBBARD's observations of a *Lyræ*, and finds that of a single observation to be but 0."155.

In the early part of the year 1849, it was my privilege to become personally acquainted with Professor HUBBARD, and to begin a friendship which knew no cloud until the last sad severance of all earthly ties. For his affectionate solicitude in time of sickness, his sympathy and support in evil days, his cordial aid in difficulty, and his encouragement in all good works, — a debt is due to his memory which words cannot express, and which, alas! this life affords no opportunity of repaying.

Without HUBBARD's cordial approval, the plan of the *Astronomical Journal* would probably not have been carried into execution ; certainly it would not, at the time when it was actually begun. He aided it in every way, — by the promise of investigations for its columns — a promise amply fulfilled; — by stimulating others both to contribute and to subscribe, — by frank criticism, by generous incitement and discriminating commendation. No one could have felt a deeper interest in it than he, and of whatever service it may have rendered, a large proportion is to be credited to him alone. The earliest letter from him in my possession, dated June 8, 1849, is almost wholly devoted to a discussion of the various plans we had previously orally debated.

In the summer of 1849, these plans were essentially matured, and after discussion with BACHE, PEIRCE, HENRY, COFFIN, WALKER, CHAUVENET, and others almost equally interested, though not themselves engaged in prosecuting the same departments of inquiry, (prominent among whom were our two honored Secretaries, and the Editors of the American Journal of Science,) it was decided to give its origin a sort of national character by causing the first public suggestion to emanate from the American Association for the Advancement of Science, which held its second session at Cambridge in August, 1849. This work HUBBARD took cordially and zealously in hand. He prepared a communication, which he laid before the Association [p. 378], representing the importance of the proposed undertaking, and the services which it might render in the development of astronomy and its kindred sciences at that critical period of our national growth. At his suggestion a committee was appointed to consider the subject, and to bring it to the notice of those interested in the advancement of astronomy. He afterwards prepared a Prospectus, and labored earnestly and with effect, for its wide circulation.

The six volumes of the Journal contain more than 210 columns of valuable contributions from his pen, — and twice during the Editor's absence from the country did HUBBARD assume the control and editorship.

3 *

The first extended computation of Professor HUBBARD consisted in the determination of the zodiacs of all the known asteroids, except the four previously published in Germany. In November, 1848, he presented to the Smithsonian Institution the Zodiacs of *Vesta, Astrea, Hebe, Flora,* and *Metis;* and to the first volume of the Astronomical Journal, he contributed those of *Hygea, Parthenope,* and *Clio,* making the list complete up to that time. That of *Egeria* followed, soon after his satisfactory determination of the elements; and although he published no others, it was his intention as well as endeavor to prepare the zodiac for each successively discovered asteroid. These zodiacs give for each planet, — as suggested by GAUSS, and computed by him for *Ceres, Pallas,* and *Juno,* — the northern and southern limits of its geocentric position for each right-ascension, and enable us in many cases to draw immediate inferences as to the possible identity of any recorded star with the planet in question. It is much to be desired that the series of asteroid-zodiacs should be completed, and a key thus furnished for the solution of many interesting questions of identity, which have occurred in the past, and must present themselves hereafter.

None of you, Gentlemen, can fail to recall the magnificent spectacle exhibited by the great Comet of 1843. Through the early evenings of March, it trailed like a gorgeous banner of flame across the Western sky, the first visitant of its kind within the memories of many a full grown man, and rekindling the awe and wonder of those, whose impressions of the cometic glories of 1807, 1811, and 1819 had become dimmed by time. Its magnificent train extended at nightfall nearly parallel with the horizon through an arc of some 40°, rivaling the later, though perhaps equally splendid, manifestation of the great Comet of 1858. So great indeed was its brilliancy while in close proximity to the sun, that it attracted the attention of the public at high noon in various parts of North and South America both on the day of its perihelion, and on the day following. It was seen at 11 o'clock on the morning of the 27th, at Conception, and measurements of its distance from the sun were made on the 28th, both in Maine and in Mexico ; the tail being visible to the length of a full degree, at 3 o'clock in the afternoon of that day. The attempts of astronomers to satisfy the observations led to results singularly diverse. Only one characteristic of the orbit seemed beyond question, — the extreme smallness of the perihelion distance. The close resemblance of its parabolic elements to those deduced by HENDERSON for the Comet of 1668, could not fail to attract attention, and the elements obtained by PEIRCE from the very unsatisfactory observations of the Comet of 1689, which have come down to us, exhibit also a decided similarity. Both CAPOCCI and CLAUSSEN, believing in its identity with both, found themselves able to satisfy the observations by an ellipse of seven years period. ENCKE, WALKER, and ANDERSON found that the observations could be closely represented by a hyperbolic orbit, — BOGUSLAWSKI in Breslau advocated a period of $147\frac{1}{2}$ years, — WALKER finally decided in favor of an ellipse of $21\frac{7}{8}$ years, — while LAUGIER and MAUVAIS in Paris, NICOLAI in Mannheim, and others, found the probabilities strongly in favor of the period of 175 years, — which I cannot but believe to be the true one.

. This magnificent object fired the zeal of HUBBARD, already fascinated as he was with astronomical study and imbued with the spirit of research. He was within five months of graduation at Yale, and, from that time, he looked forward to a thorough and decisive investigation of the path of this comet, as his most favorite problem. And although some six years elapsed before he found it within his power to begin the long-desired research, he then prosecuted it with an earnestness which showed no loss of interest or of enthusiasm.

In December, 1849, he published the first part of this masterly discussion of the Orbit of the Great Comet of 1843, — an investigation begun only a few months before, but hastened for the sake of an early contribution to the Astronomical Journal. This paper occupied a part of eight numbers, the conclusion appearing in July, 1852. It seems to me safe to say that the orbit of no comet of long period has been more thoroughly and exhaustively treated than this. All observations of the comet, of whatever kind, whether before published or obtained from the manuscripts of astronomers, were subjected to rigorous scrutiny, and were winnowed with a painstaking fidelity which would have surpassed the patience of most men. Especially were the very important sextant-observations, made in the daytime on the 28th of February by Captain CLARKE, at Portland, Maine, and by Mr. BOWRING, at Chihuahua, discussed with extreme care, and made, after sundry corrections, to exert an important influence upon the resultant orbit.

First forming normal places by the aid of one of the approximate parabolas at hand, HUBBARD computed elliptic elements by the ordinary Gaussian method, and thus obtained new normals. Determining for these the coefficients of the variations of the elements relatively to the variations of the geocentric co-ordinates, — and, for the sake of control, both by BESSEL's method and by that of GOETZE, he deduced the variations required for satisfying the new normals, and thus arrived at a second set of elements.

Repeating the process, and computing ten new equations

of condition for new normal places, he obtained a third and fourth ellipse, the latter by the assignment of weights to the several normals. The amount of outstanding error was thus reduced to a very small quantity, and the orbit was sufficiently accurate to correct the sextant-observations, and decide sundry points left ambiguous by the observer. Thus he found which limit of the sun had been compared with the comet at Chihuahua, and was able to make the assumption of an error of two minutes in one of the recorded times of observation, and thus both to render the observations accordant, and to show their value. In a similar way the untrustworthiness of another sextant-observation was made manifest, and thus prevented from vitiating the computations. The errors of two sextant-measurements in each place were thus shown to lie within the limits of good observation, and the aid of these very important auxiliaries secured.

The disturbing forces were computed for each of the six large planets for each fourth day during the period of the comet's visibility, and with the series of osculating elements thus obtained, he determined the discordances of every accessible observation. Here, as everywhere in HUBBARD's work, we find the indication of his scrupulous care in controlling his computations by the independent employment of different formulas, and of the tact by which he adapted various methods to his purpose; this peculiarity, as well as his exquisite elegance in the mechanical arrangement, and the beauty of his chirography reminding one continually of ENCKE, many of whose scientific characteristics seem equally to have belonged to HUBBARD, — though the fulness of years and opportunities happily accorded to the accomplished astronomer of Berlin were denied to our departed associate. True to his nature, he computed all the anomalies and radius-vectors in duplicate, once by means of a manuscript table to supply the reductions needed for NICOLAI's formulas, which proved more convenient than BARKER's table for an orbit of so small a perihelion distance, and then again by means of the Besselian reduction of the parabola to an ellipse.

New equations of condition were now formed, sixty-six in number, — weights were empirically assigned to each, and a fifth system of elements thus found which absolutely represented the Portland observation, and satisfied the two Chihuahua altitudes so admirably that the greatest discordance of the five amounted to but 37″, while the probable error of a normal place amounted to 16″. Separating the observations made with a ring-micrometer from those obtained by the filar micrometer, he was able to assign more accurate weights to the several measurements of each coordinate, and found, as might have been anticipated, that the probable error with the ring-micrometer did not much exceed that with the filar micrometer for differences of right ascension, while it proved to be nearly in the ratio of 7 to 10 for differences of declination.

By a repetition of the process, after assigning carefully computed weights, as above mentioned, to sixty-five normal equations of condition, HUBBARD obtained by the method of least squares a sixth system of elements, which gave the best possible representation to the entire series of observations, and reduced the probable error of a normal place to
. less than 13″.

Here the investigation might well have rested; for the effect of terms of the second order, both in the perturbations and in the comparisons, might fairly be considered as removed, and the sums of the squares of the residuals were a minimum. But HUBBARD was not content to leave any

investigation, where there seemed an opportunity of prosecuting it further with success; and since the incorporation
of observations made with the ring-micrometer had increased the probable errors of the results, and since the
series with the filar micrometer extended through the whole
period of visibility excepting the observations by daylight,
he passed on to still another determination from the filar-
micrometer observations alone combined with the sextant-
observations of February 28. From these he constructed
eighty-three new equations of condition, determined a
seventh series of elements, reducing the probable error
of a single normal to less than $8''.5$, and assigned for each
element its probable error. The period corresponding to
these final elements was somewhat more than five hundred
years, and it became a problem of much interest to determine to what extent the resultant period might be varied
consistently with the probable limits of errors of observation. This HUBBARD solved most thoroughly by an ingeni-
ous method of determining the variations of each of the
elements, of the probable errors, and of each normal place,
as a function of the variation of the eccentricity. So that
by substituting in these expressions the change of eccentricity corresponding to any suspected period, a few minutes of
figuring will give us the corresponding elements, the probable error of normal places, and the individual discordances
of observations. This substitution he carried out himself
for the period of one hundred and seventy-five years, and
found that it implied a probable error of $11''\frac{1}{3}$ for a single
observation, and no individual discordances beyond the limit
of reasonable error; although, to be sure, a certain " rate "
seems indicated on this assumption by the earlier observations. The limits of periodic time consistent with its observed geocentric path were thus shown to be extremely

wide; and HUBBARD closed by suggesting that the want of coincidence between the centre of gravity and the centre of apparent condensation, as well as the operation of polar forces in the comet itself, might perhaps modify deductions drawn without consideration of these possible influences.

I have not hesitated, Gentlemen of the Academy, to describe this valuable memoir with a minuteness of detail quite unsuitable for a popular address; both because its masterly completeness and elegance render it a model investigation of its class, and because these qualities were so characteristic of our late colleague that a somewhat minute description seemed well adapted to exhibit his habits of mind and mode of research. Preserved in the Library of Yale College are three quarto volumes containing the actual numerical computations, — all executed with marvellous neatness and a beauty of penmanship approaching the elegance of copperplate engraving, — all arranged in due order, and in the form most convenient for reference, and all bearing the strong impress of the man. Indeed, in every one of his manuscripts we may see the reflection of his own cultivated and tasteful mind, in which there was no slovenly corner, or ill-finished record.

HUBBARD's next investigation of magnitude was upon Biela's comet. Four quarto volumes, filled with neat figures, lie before me as I write, containing his researches concerning the orbit of this most interesting body. They are a priceless and treasured memento of our departed friend, which I owe to the thoughtful kindness of his family; and it is not improbable that four or five years hence they may facilitate the discovery of the origin and nature of the mysterious transformations which this singular comet has undergone, and may aid in the detection of the unknown laws controlling its physical structure.

It is known to you all that Biela's comet, as it is generally called, is one of short period, performing its entire revolution in about $6\frac{3}{4}$ years. It was first seen in 1772, by MONTAIGNE, who made three or four imperfect and untrustworthy estimates of position, and it was observed four times, quite unsatisfactorily, by MESSIER. In 1806, it was detected by PONS; and the general resemblance of its orbit to the approximate one deduced for the comet of 1772, attracted immediate attention. BESSEL and GAUSS computed elliptic orbits on the supposition of identity. The latter found the apparent path as well represented by an ellipse of $4\frac{3}{4}$ years as by his best parabola, thus suggesting the probability that there had been six intermediate returns. The places observed in 1772 were, however, not so well satisfied by an ellipse of so short a major axis, and therefore while the hypothesis of identity seemed plausible, it could hardly be considered probable. It was not until 1826 that the comet was seen again. In that year it was independently discovered both on the 27th February, by VON BIELA, an Austrian captain, on duty at the fortress of Josephstadt, and by GAMBART in Marseilles, ten days later. Upon the first computation of the orbit, each recognized the identity of the comet with that of 1806, and the true length of the period became manifest.

The next return, in 1832, was successfully predicted by astronomers; at the following one in 1839, it was not discovered; and in the winter of 1845 – 6, a predicted return was for the second time observed. But here an unexpected and anomalous phenomenon was exhibited. The comet, which was detected at the close of November, was before the end of December seen to be double, and the two components became apparently farther and farther apart, until, at the end of March, their distance from one another amounted to more than 14′.

It was of course immediately maintained by some that an explosion had occurred, and it became a question of great interest to all astronomers, when, how, and through what agency the separation had been brought about. And yet another curious circumstance was this : — that whereas the northern and preceding component was at first so decidedly the fainter of the two as to receive the name of the " companion," while the southerly one was regarded as the comet proper ; — yet this companion, or northerly component, gradually increased in brilliancy, until about the time of perihelion-passage, surpassing the primary nucleus for several days, and then again diminishing in relative brightness so long as observations could be made.

HUBBARD, who had observed this comet at Washington early in January, 1846, had been deeply impressed with these inexplicable phenomena, and no astronomer looked forward to its return in 1852 with more anxious interest than he. Would two independent comets be found traversing the same path ? or would the phenomenon of a double nucleus be again exhibited ? or would the two components manifest mutual relations analogous to those of satellite and primary, or at least to those of binary stars ? Would it be possible for observations of each component at the coming perihelion passage to be combined with those made at the last return, so that an ellipse could be deduced for each, and the point of intersection thus determined ? These and many similar queries were often discussed ; and immediately on the completion of his paper on the comet of 1843, he began his preparations for an equally thorough investigation of Biela's comet so soon as its approaching return to the sun should have been thoroughly observed.

For a month previous to the detection of the comet, HUBBARD had been engaged in the preparation of an ephemeris to insure its discovery at as early a date as possible, and had succeeded in obtaining an orbit decidedly better than SAN-TINI's, which was the best existing. But the discovery of the comet rendered the publication of this ephemeris unnecessary.

On the 26th August, 1852, Father SECCHI, at Rome, while searching for Biela's comet in the neighborhood of the place indicated by SANTINI's ephemeris, discovered a very faint nebulous comet somewhat more than $4\frac{1}{2}°$ from the place predicted for Biela's, and was able to fix its position with great accuracy by its transit over a small star of the 9.10 magnitude, which it covered at one time so centrally that the comet could only be recognized by the circumstance that the star seemed enveloped in a faint nebulosity. "I do not know," he adds, "whether this is a new comet or a portion of Biela's which was divided in the beginning of 1846."

There seemed but little room for reasonable doubt that this was really Biela's comet, or one of its component parts; since its position, though varying from the ephemeris, was nearly in the same orbit, and the amount and direction of its motion were what might have been expected. But all doubt was removed three weeks later, when Professor SECCHI detected the other portion of the comet, following its predecessor by about half a degree of right-ascension, and about half a degree farther south, and fainter even than the other. Owing to this extreme faintness of both portions, observations could only be continued for a little more than ten days after the discovery of the second component. The last return to perihelion took place in 1859, but the position of the comet was so unfavorable, that although ephemerides prepared by three independent computers, one of them HUBBARD himself, agreed very closely, and the most powerful telescopes of the world were occupied in the search, the comet was not seen.

With this brief sketch of the history of our knowledge of Biela's comet, I may, without entering into close detail, describe HUBBARD's labors and researches concerning it. His published Memoirs on this subject are three in number, in addition to sundry smaller communications on special points; such as one in which he corrected a serious error, which had found its way into the best European computations of the perturbations in 1845 – 6, and explained its probable origin; and a publication of the valuable manuscript observations made by Professor CHALLIS in Cambridge, England, during the same period, and sent by this distinguished astronomer to Professor HUBBARD for employment in his investigations.

The first of these Memoirs is entitled, "On the Orbit of Biela's Comet in 1845 – 6." In this, as in every other memoir of its author, the same searching thoroughness and scrupulous accuracy are manifest which I have recounted concerning his investigation on the comet of 1843. All known observations were employed, no appreciable refinement of method or computation was neglected; and the materials were so fully and completely discussed that it is improbable that any results can ever be drawn from them which he did not himself deduce. The principal results of this memoir, in addition to the discussion of all the observations, consisted in the definite determination of elements for each component, together with their variations for any variation of the adopted mean motion; and in the discovery that by far the greater part of the difference between the two orbits might be represented by a variation in the mean anomaly alone. The residual errors implied by this assumption are very small, much less than the errors of individual observations, and in no case exceeding 8″; but they are nevertheless too symmetric, and too large for his normal places, and he points out, moreover, that some difference must necessarily exist in the mean motions.

In a letter of about this date (1853, June 8), he writes, jestingly: " Biela slides on smoothly. I don't work now, as on '43, wearily and with a $D\psi$, nor boldly and with $D\phi$ance $D\Omega$ing a change of Inclination, but $D\mu$rely. An allowable change of 0.″34 in the mean motion will give the places in 1852, within 24″ + the error of Santini's perturbations, provided I am right in assigning the nuclei relatively to each other; but it is not so easy to tell which is which, as I had supposed."

Hubbard's published investigations reached this point in the summer of 1853 ; and he was leisurely preparing the materials for a continuance of the work, when the Imperial Academy of Sciences of St.-Petersburg, in December of that year, offered its astronomical prize for just such an investigation as that on which he was engaged. The distinguished head of the Observatory at Pulkowa wrote specially to suggest the publication in the United States of the Programme for the prize ; and it may well be suspected that the very able discussion which Hubbard had already given might, at least in some degree, have tended to assure the astronomers of the Imperial Academy that competent men were already enlisted in the investigation, whom the liberal prize might at once stimulate and reward. And in view of the laborious and extended computations, which the solution of the problem would entail, a period of nearly four years was allowed for the preparation of the memoir. Many of Hubbard's friends desired him to compete for this prize, which I think there is no reasonable doubt would have been won by the memoirs which he subsequently published in America.

But Hubbard's delicate health, together with his earnest

desire that whatever he might do for science should inure to his own country's service, prevented him from yielding to the temptation. He considered the matter for a brief period, and then decided that he " ought not to work against time," and the close of his researches was not reached till 1860. The second paper, published in July, 1854, is entitled, " Results of additional Investigations respecting the two Nuclei of Biela's Comet." In this short, but very elaborate and important memoir, HUBBARD discussed the observations of each nucleus in 1852, determining elements for each. And he arrived at the very remarkable results which seem now incontestable, " that notwithstanding the increased mutual distance of the two nuclei, their alternation, of relative brilliancy were much greater than those noticed in 1846; so great indeed, for several days, as to amount to alternations of visibility from day to day "; and that the observations at Berlin, 1845, November 29 and December 2, were of the primary nucleus, the second being invisible to the observers; while those of CHALLIS, December 1 and 3, were of the secondary, the first being unseen. So that it is clear, both that we are in possession of observations of the second nucleus, made in the beginning of December, 1845, before the existence of two nuclei was suspected, and that even at that time occurred those singular alternations of light which were repeated in 1852. Furthermore, he made it highly probable that the preceding component, in 1846, was identical with the following one in 1852, and *vice versâ*; and finally, that the separation of the nuclei must have occurred not far from 316° of heliocentric longitude, corresponding to a time about five hundred days before the perihelion passage of 1846.

At the close of 1858, HUBBARD published a short papers containing a condensed notice of the condition of the prob

lem, together with new elements for each nucleus, and an
ephemeris for each at the approaching return of the comet
to perihelion. This I have not counted as one of the Memoirs. His third and last paper on the subject appeared in
May, 1860, under the title, "On Biela's Comet." It con-
sists first of an admirable history of all our knowledge of
this comet, with full references to the original sources, and
presents an excellent specimen of what might be called condensed detail. Next it contains an elaborate discussion of
the observations and orbit for every recorded appearance.
And in the discussion of the last appearance in 1852, he
brought to light a new illustration of the mysterious alternation of brilliancy between the two nuclei. For he showed,
that when, on the 15th of September, SECCHI found both
nuclei, and determined the position of one of them, the new
one being too faint for observation, this so-called "new
one" was the identical nucleus which he had discovered
in August, and had been observing ever since; while the
brighter of the two had then just become visible. "On the
16th, the southern nucleus alone was visible; on the 17th
and 18th, only the northern; and finally, on the 19th, both
were observed by SECCHI. The double observation was
repeated at Rome and at Pulkowa, on the 20th, 23d, and
25th; while on the 21st only the southern, and on the 22d
only the northern, was visible. We thus have a most interesting repetition of the alternations in 1845 – 6, which
now appear more remarkable only in consequence of the
extreme faintness of the comets, which was such, that the
slightest change of light sufficed to carry them within or
beyond the scope of vision." (*Astron. Journal*, VI. 140.)

Finally, a recapitulation of the final elements for each
nucleus, and for all the observations and normal places, ex-
hausts the sum of our present knowledge of Biela's comet,

. and leaves us ready for the new investigations which its return eighteen months hence will require.

Another extended investigation by HUBBARD is that upon the Fourth Comet of 1825. HANSEN had long ago found that the observations before and after perihelion seemed better reconciled by an ellipse than by a parabola; and HUBBARD undertook the collection and discussion of all the observations in the hope of some definite determination of the major axis. This investigation occupied much of his time at irregular intervals for five or six years, and was finally published in the spring of 1859. In this, as in most of these cometary investigations, a leading object was to learn whether the motions of the comets, distinguished by their magnitude or varying aspect, or by any other striking peculiarity, would prove in all cases amenable to the law of gravitation alone. In the case of the comet of 1825, no special fact of general interest was elicited; but negative results, though less interesting, are attained with no less labor and skill than positive ones, and are often scarcely less important. Suffice it to say of this memoir, that it is complete, and apparently exhaustive; that the elliptic character of the comet is fully demonstrated, although its periodic time must be exceedingly long; and the material deducible from past observation lies ready for the hands of the future investigator.

I have now spoken, Gentlemen, at sufficient length of the larger and more extended memoirs of our departed colleague, and have described their characteristic features. Of his minor contributions to astronomy I need say no more than that they resembled the larger ones in thoroughness and neatness of conception. The columns of the Astronomical Journal, and the pages of the Washington Observations, are full of them: — elements and ephemerides of many a

comet and many an asteroid, elegant and appropriate sugges-
tions, generally relating to methods of computation, or in-
genious devices for attaining a desired end with economy
of labor.

In the excellent tables appended by Professor COFFIN
and himself to several volumes of the Washington Observations; in the reduction and discussion of the geographical
observations made by Lieutenants (now Major-Generals)
FRÉMONT and EMORY on their various expeditions; in the
thorough investigations of the several instruments successively placed in his charge, — the accuracy and conscientious-
ness of HUBBARD still·bear fruit for us.

One of his latest labors was an unpublished investigation
of the magnetism of iron vessels, and its effect upon the com-
pass, — upon which he was employed nearly to the time when
a Permanent Commission appointed by the Navy Department
undertook the same research upon that more extended scale,
which the same gentlemen have continued till the present
time in the form of a committee of the National Academy.

No description of HUBBARD's intellectual character could
be regarded as complete, that omitted one predominant trait
which pervaded all his opinions, and lay deeply rooted in
the very foundations of his nature. I mean that deep love
of truth and loathing of all false assumption, which may be
said to bear the same relation to honesty that honesty bears
to what is called " worldly policy." There were few things
which his modest and tolerant spirit could be said to hate;
but he did hate sham, humbug, and charlatanism with all
the energy of his soul. He never claimed honor, rank, or
position for himself, although he hastened to accord all these
to others far less worthy than he ; but he was restive at the
sight of scientific rewards unworthily bestowed by incom-
petent tribunals; and his sterling patriotism and sense of
justice not unfrequently united in paining him, when —

> " He saw the holy wreaths of Fame
> Profaned to deck ignoble brows."

Thus far, gentlemen, I have endeavored to describe Professor HUBBARD to you as a man of science, — showing you the early efforts of his mind, and the eager pursuit of knowledge which characterized even his boyhood. We have seen what he had accomplished at the age of thirty-nine; and alas! how much more he promised for the future which we hoped for him. But though all this is done, I feel that the more difficult part of my duty to his memory remains undone; and I approach it with yet greater distrust of my ability to do it aright. It is comparatively an easy task to trace the working of his mind, and the results of his studies; but to show him as some of us knew him, as a son, a brother, a friend, a Christian, to do him justice without trespassing on that privacy which none valued more highly than he, requires a hand of equal delicacy and skill. One assistance at least the biographer of HUBBARD may justly feel to be accorded him, — that in that life there is no record to be concealed, no page to be glanced at and quickly closed with pain. His only choice is what to show, not what to hide.

Our colleague had a kindly, gentle nature, and an affectionate regard for all around him. He made his own opportunities to help and cheer others, instead of waiting for them. Was a friend successful, he rejoiced with a cordiality that made him twice happy; in sorrow, he mourned with him, and with a sympathy that half lifted off the burden. One of the strongest affections of his life was for his mother. He showed her not only the natural affection and tenderness of a son, the respect due from youth to honorable age, or the attachment which old and cherished associations awaken, but to the very last he made her his confidante and counselor. His deepest thoughts and highest aspirations, his struggles and his joys, were alike intrusted to her; a precious deposit, which her heart knew how to keep and ponder.

Professor HUBBARD was married at the age of twenty-five to Miss SARAH E. L. HANDY of Washington, on the 27th of April, 1848. Few men were more fitted than he to enjoy the comforts of a home, or could better appreciate the blessings of his new relation; but there were many clouds to overshadow the horizon, as he himself says in one short note, whose pathos only those can understand who know that it was but once or twice in a lifetime that a murmur escaped his lips. Upon the threshold of his home stood always that dreary visitant, Ill-health, whose dominion over both mental and physical content most of us know too well. HUBBARD'S own health was never certain, but his wife was a far greater sufferer; and often, unknown to herself, her troubles weighed too heavily upon his over-tasked mind and sensitive heart. Even pecuniary embarrassments, those petty cares that, unlike deeper sorrows, fail to brace the mind they attack, were not wanting to sting his delicate and generous spirit. Each day their peculiar circumstances compelled new outlays, to be defrayed only from means already too slender. We can appreciate their struggles, without prying too closely into what he might have wished forgotten. We can see the student compelled to forego his cherished pursuits, the man of tender sensitiveness wrung by the sufferings of those nearest him, the invalid whose frail health varied with each new trial. We can see all this; but to a spirit such as his must have come many a compensation, many a blessing won from the dark angels by bitter wrestling.

> " For that high suffering which we dread
>   A higher joy discloses;
> Men see the thorns on Jesus' head,
>   But angels see the roses."

After eight and a half years of married life, a long desired change came to the little household, and with a new joy he welcomed his child. With what hope and happiness he accepted the new promise, those who knew him well cannot forget; but the happiness was all too short. " The little spirit only fluttered for a while on the threshold of its prison-house, and unconscious of captivity took flight forever." Writing to a near friend at the time, HUBBARD says, " God bless you for the interest you took in my boy. This is all I can say; for I cannot write of him." Nor will I undertake to speak of his grief. Four years later, Mrs. HUBBARD's suffering life terminated; and her husband was left alone, with only the remembrance of a home.

As a friend I knew HUBBARD well, and can bear witness to the loyalty and gentleness of his nature. With a gayety never bordering on excess, a sympathy never exhausted, a kindly tact never forgotten, he was a companion such as we rarely meet. Of his help and encouragement to me personally, I have already spoken ; and since I have read the memorials entrusted to my care, I see that what he did for me he did for many others, each according to his need.

During the last few years of our colleague's life, there seems to have been some modification, or at least exaltation, of the views and sentiments which, perhaps more than any others, tend to make each one of us what we are, — I mean our sense of personal relation to the Deity. That high principle and religious fervor which through his life had been a lamp to his feet, showing itself in love to God and man, burnt during these later years with a yet brighter flame. Perhaps, indeed, it may to some of us seem for a moment to have dazzled his vision, and made the shadows which must darken every thoughtful mind seem blacker than those ordained by the hand of a loving Father. In reading these last memorials, we cannot but grieve that his pure and gentle spirit should have passed through those hours of struggle which, to our vision at least, he seemed to need so little. But it is not for us to scan too closely the sacred privacy of these emotions. Let us turn rather to their results.

He was long connected with the religious society of Rev. Dr. GURLEY, in Washington; and his letters to his mother show the reliance which he placed upon this excellent man, and the eagerness with which he sought to know and do his Master's will. He became an elder of the church, and not many months before his death, Superintendent of the Sunday Schools of the Presbyterian denomination in the city. In the affections and lives of his associates and pupils, we find the best tribute to the ability and fidelity with which he discharged these duties.

Among the writings of these later months are various treatises on religious and theological subjects, and critical comparisons and reconciliations of various portions of the Old and New Testaments; to all of which he brought the same power of unwearying research that characterized his scientific labors. He attempted the mastery of the Hebrew language, and labored zealously to fit himself for a more critical study of the Bible. Indeed so earnest was his religious devotion that we find indications of some vague aspiration, or half-formed plan, of renouncing even his scientific pursuits in order to enter upon the labors of the Christian ministry. To each one is intrusted his peculiar gift; and we who knew HUBBARD as a student and minister of science, cannot but feel that his Maker had clearly pointed out the way in which he best might serve Him, by devoting a rare capacity and pure heart to the study and interpretation of His works.

5

Perhaps, Gentlemen, we may regret that, even for a moment, and from the highest possible motives, he was unfaithful to his earliest choice, and swerved from the path where, as we think, he best served God and man. Yet such questions must be decided by every man for himself, with such light as he may attain; and it may be that these varied experiences and changes of thought were sent him that he might live through the experience of many years during the lapse of a few, and might learn as many as possible of the lessons of this life during the time allotted him. But can we do otherwise than honor a creed which blossoms in such deeds as crowded the last years of HUBBARD's life. His was no bigot's zeal. It led him among the poor, the sick, and the afflicted. It sent him to the hospitals, where he daily spent his hours of official leisure with the soldiers, giving each the needful word of good cheer, or bringing delicacies and comforts to them so far as his own opportunities or those of his friends permitted. It inspired him with a true loyalty to his country, and endowed him with that spirit of self-sacrifice which shone in every action. "The number of letters that he wrote for wounded soldiers," says a friend in writing of him, "was almost incredible. He frequently devoted whole afternoons to this one object. I wonder how many of the soldiers knew whose bright face it was that was so pleasant to them."

With all these self-imposed duties added to his daily and nightly routine of work, who can wonder that his health, always so uncertain, became each month still more impaired; and that when the last summons came it was so quickly answered.

Professor HUBBARD left Washington for the last time on the 30th July, 1863. For a few days previous he had been particularly unwell, owing to severe exposure in a sudden

shower. But he had looked forward with peculiar pleasure
to a meeting of his college classmates in celebration of the
twentieth anniversary of their graduation ; and he managed
to pursue his original plan, and reached New Haven in time
for the meeting. But the delicate instrument had been too
much shattered to recover its tone, and its music was to be
heard no longer. He suffered severely on the journey, and
on being assisted into the well-remembered house where his
mother was awaiting him, had only strength to say, " O, how
good it is to be at home." His mother pressed forward to
meet him, and he added those words, which to our ears seem
so full of pathos : " Mother, I am worn out."

And so indeed it proved. To the physician who was in-
stantly summoned, he only said : " Doctor, help me to a little
strength to meet my class to-morrow night, and then I will
give up." But even this gratification was denied him, and
the affectionate greeting that he sent his classmates was almost his last earthly utterance. Gradually, but surely, he
sank away ; but who could have wished for him a happier
dismissal ? Soothed by familiar voices and pleasant images,
tended as in his infancy by his mother, surrounded by loving
faces, the worn-out man may have felt himself a weary child
again ; and with a childlike confidence he went to rest, on
Sunday morning, August 16, — waking, we may be sure, to
exclaim once more, " How good it is to be at home." A
day or two afterward his mortal part was laid in the quiet
cemetery near us, where, two years before, that very week,
he had seen his father laid.

" Sleep sweetly, tender heart, in peace;
Sleep, holy spirit, blessed soul,
While the stars burn, the moons increase,
And the great ages onward roll.

" Sleep till the end, true soul and sweet,
Nothing comes to thee new or strange;

Sleep, full of rest from head to feet;
Lie still, dry dust, secure of change."

Here we leave him. But, gentlemen of the National
Academy, let not the name of the first who left our ranks be
soon forgotten. Others of those ranks may have emblazoned
their names more conspicuously, their memory may be yet
more secure of perpetuity, in the annals of science. But
none of our number can claim to have surpassed him in those
qualities which make the highest glory of a man; and well
will it be for us if our names can be inscribed near his, on
the highest of records.

If our National Academy is to fulfil its loftiest mission,
and achieve a work commensurate with our hope and faith,
let us emulate the spirit of him whom we have first been
called upon to mourn. — the spirit of disinterestedness, of
patriotism, and of highest purpose.

Cambridge: Printed by Welch, Bigelow, & Co.